Cool Kid Inventions

Laura Hamilton Waxman

Lerner Publications • Minneapolis

To Nathan, whose mind is always wandering about and dreaming up new things —L.H.W.

Lerner Publications Company
An imprint of Lerner Publishing Group, Inc.
241 First Avenue North
Minneapolis, MN 55401 USA

For reading levels and more information, look up this title at www.lernerbooks.com.

Library of Congress Cataloging-in-Publication Data

Names: Waxman, Laura Hamilton, author.
Title: Cool kid inventions / Laura Hamilton Waxman.
Description: Minneapolis, MN : Lerner Publications Company, 2020. | Series: Lightning Bolt Books. Kids in Charge! | Includes bibliographical references and index. | Audience: Age 6-9. | Audience: Grade K to 3.
Identifiers: LCCN 2019017248 (print) | LCCN 2019020589 (ebook) | ISBN 9781541583214 (eb pdf) | ISBN 9781541576995 (lb : alk. paper) | ISBN 9781541589124 (pb : alk. paper)
Subjects: LCSH: Inventions—Juvenile literature. | Children as inventors—Juvenile literature.
Classification: LCC T212 (ebook) | LCC T212 .W39 2020 (print) | DDC 600—dc23

LC record available at https://lccn.loc.gov/2019017248

Manufactured in the United States of America
2 - 51709 - 47712 - 2/25/2022

Table of Contents

Kids with Big Ideas

Do you like to dream up new things? Maybe you want to solve a problem or help people. That's what kid inventors do!

Some inventors get awards for their creative ideas.

Kid inventors have cool ideas. They work hard to turn those ideas into something real. Their inventions change people's lives.

Blast from the Past

Some kid inventions are made to last. Think of ice pops and trampolines. They were dreamed up years ago by kids!

Robert Patch

The toy truck is a kid invention from the past. A boy named Robert Patch designed it when he was five in 1962. With the help of his dad, he got a US patent for his toy truck the next year.

Robert made his first truck with some shoeboxes, bottle caps, and nails.

Louis Braille

Have you heard of an invention called braille? It allows the blind to read and write. Braille uses raised dots that people can read with their fingers.

The invention was named after its young inventor. Louis Braille was a blind child who was born in 1809. He invented braille to make it easier for him and other blind people to read.

You can find braille on signs, in books, and on elevator buttons.

Cool Stuff by Kids

Have you ever thought of a cool idea? These inventors sure have. Their inventions solve big problems.

Kiowa Kavovit

Kiowa Kavovit was four when she created Boo Boo Goo. It covers cuts and helps them heal. Boo Boo Goo does not fall off like a bandage might.

Boo Boo Goo is painted on and sticks to your skin.

Bishop Curry

Bishop Curry's invention keeps babies safe. It senses when a baby is left alone in a hot car. Then it blows cool air on the baby. It also calls the parents or the police for help.

Bishop's invention Oasis protects babies.

Amelia Fox

At eight years old, Amelia Fox invented a wheelchair hoist. It lifts a person out of a wheelchair. Amelia designed it to help people like her brother, Jake.

Amelia's hoist helps people who use wheelchairs.

Creating Fun

Ellie Skalla

Inventors like Ellie Skalla add fun to people's lives. Ellie won a young inventor's contest for her board game GalactiQuest. The game takes players on an adventure into outer space.

In *GalactiQuest*, players take over as many planets as they can.

Jakob Sperry

Jakob Sperry's invention is fun and useful. His GyRings are small, handheld toys. They help people stay calm and focused.

Like GyRings, fidget spinners help people focus.

Cool Scientists and Coders

Do you like science and technology? Some inventors use science and coding to create new technology.

Gitanjali Rao

Lead is a natural metal. But water with lead in it is not safe to drink. Gitanjali Rao's tool, Tethys, shows if water has lead in it.

Gitanjali speaks at an invention conference.

Cassandra and Caitlyn demonstrate their invention at the White House Science Fair.

Texas Tweens

In Texas, Cassandra Baquero, Caitlyn Gonzalez, and their four friends wanted to help a blind classmate find new places. So they wrote the code for Hello Navi. This phone app gives spoken directions.

Inventors like Caitlyn Gonzalez, Bishop Curry, and Kiowa Kavovit are making a difference. They're getting creative and working hard. They're changing the world one invention at a time.

You Can Do It!

Do you want to be an inventor? Start by asking, what problem in the world do I want to solve?

Maybe you want to help people or animals. Maybe you just want to make life more fun. Learn all you can about the problem. Then think about an invention that could help solve it. Check out the Further Reading list on page 23 to learn more about inventing and inventors.

Did You Know?

- Toy truck inventor Robert Patch was the youngest American to get a US patent.

- Amelia Fox's wheelchair hoist won her a trip to NASA (the National Aeronautics and Space Administration).

- Eight-year-old Abbey Fleck created an easier way to cook bacon with the Makin Bacon dish. She has sold more than 2.7 million Makin Bacons.

Glossary

app: a computer program made for cell phones and tablets

braille: raised dots on a page that allow people to read with their sense of touch

code: directions that computers, phones, and tablets can understand

design: to make a plan for how something will look and work

hoist: a tool that lifts something

lead: a gray metal that is found deep underground and that is used for making things

patent: a government paper saying that no one can copy an inventor's idea for a certain number of years

technology: new tools or machines that change how people live

Further Reading

Inventions by Kids
https://www.cnbc.com/id/44719456

Inventive Kids
http://inventivekids.com

Jones, Charlotte Foltz. *Mistakes That Worked: The World's Familiar Inventions and How They Came to Be*. New York: Delacorte, 2016.

Kid Inventors' Day: Tips for Kid Inventors
http://kidinventorsday.com/tips_for_kids.htm

Rhatigan, Joe. *Wacky Inventions throughout History: Weird Inventions that Seem Too Crazy to be Real!* Lake Forest, CA: Walter Foster Jr., 2018.

United States Patent and Trademark Office for Kids
https://www.uspto.gov/kids/kids.html

Index

Photo Acknowledgments

Image credits: pearleye/Getty Images, p. 2; Alina555/Getty Images, p. 4; Luiz Rampelotto/ EuropaNewswire/AP Images, p. 5; selkus/Getty Images, p. 6; AP Photo/Washington Post, p. 7; Phanie/Alamy Stock Photo, p. 8; wavebreakmedia/Shutterstock.com, p. 9; Maskot/ Getty Images, p. 10; Ravi Ranjan/Getty Images, p. 11; Chris Tobin/Getty Images, p. 12; ClarkandCompany/Getty Images, p. 13; Maximusnd/Getty Images, p. 14; Antonio Gravante/ Shutterstock.com, p. 15; Ellica/Shutterstock.com, p. 16; Rachel Murray/Stringer/Getty Images, p. 17; AP Photo/Evan Vucci, p. 18; asiseeit/Getty Images, p. 19; Art Directors & TRIP/ Alamy Stock Photo, p. 23.

Cover Image: Kathryn Scott/Getty Images.

Main body text set in Billy Infant regular. Typeface provided by SparkType.